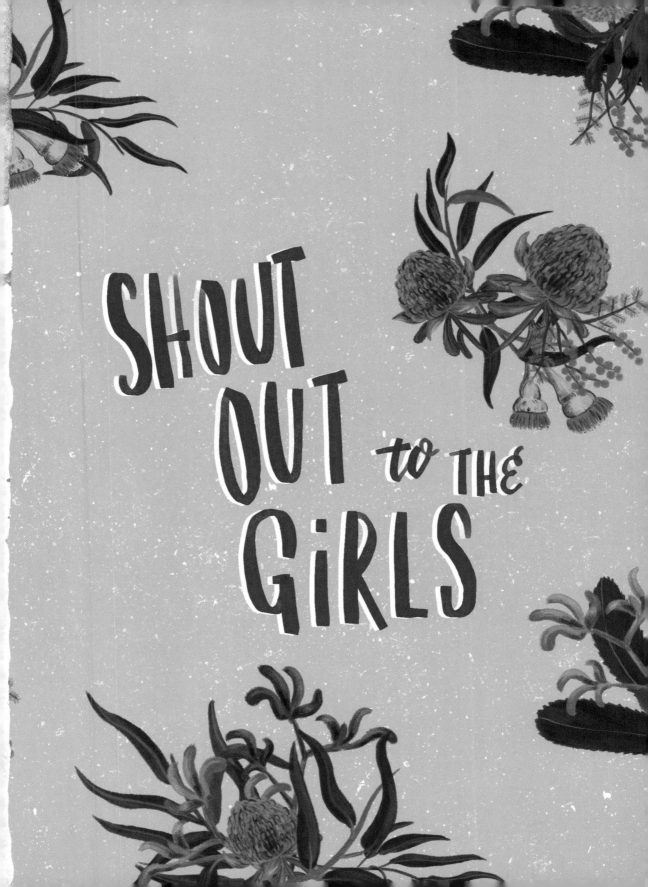

SHOUT OUT to THE GIRLS

A CELEBRATION OF AWESOME AUSTRALIAN WOMEN

RANDOM HOUSE AUSTRALIA

A Random House book
Published by Penguin Random House Australia Pty Ltd
Level 3, 100 Pacific Highway, North Sydney NSW 2060
www.penguin.com.au

Penguin
Random House
Australia

First published by Random House Australia in 2018

Addresses for the Penguin Random House group of companies can be found at
global.penguinrandomhouse.com/offices.

National Library of Australia
Cataloguing-in-Publication entry

Title: Shout out to the girls: a celebration of awesome Australian women / Various
ISBN: 978 0 14378 942 0 (hardback)
Subjects: Women – Australia – Biography
         Women in public life – Australia – Biography
         Women executives – Australia – Biography
         Women athletes – Australia – Biography

Cover and internal design by Astred Hicks, Design Cherry
Printed in China

Penguin Random House Australia uses papers that are natural, renewable and
recyclable products and made from wood grown in sustainable forests. The logging
and manufacturing processes are expected to conform to the environmental
regulations of the country of origin.

Every effort has been made to ensure that the facts presented in this book are correct.
Please contact the publisher regarding any errors to ensure they are rectified in
subsequent editions. Please also note that the biographies of the featured women are
not encyclopedic accounts of their lives and accomplishments.

Aboriginal and Torres Strait Islander readers are advised that this book contains
images and names of deceased persons.

SHOUT-OUT

noun, colloquial
a public expression of thanks

CONTENTS

Inside this book you will find women from Australia's past and present; women who are well known and some who are not so well known; women who represent a wide variety of backgrounds, accomplishments and industries; women who are young and awesome, or with a lifetime of amazingness.

Above all, you will find women to be proud of!

SHOUT OUT to THE GiRLS

A SHOUT-OUT TO

AHEDA ZANETTI

FOR HER CREATIVE INGENUITY

A pat on the back
to all the excellent
entrepreneurs
taking chances
and thinking
outside the box.

AHEDA ZANETTI

(1967–)

Aheda Zanetti and her family moved from Lebanon to Sydney when she was two years old.

Like many Muslim women raised in the West, Aheda wanted to adhere to Islamic clothing norms while also keeping up with Western fashion, especially when it came to activewear. It was after watching her niece struggle to play netball with her sporting uniform worn on top of her religious clothing that an idea came to Aheda. She was going to create a garment that combined Islamic modesty with Australian beach and sporting culture.

After many months perfecting her designs, Aheda unveiled the hijood and the burkini. Both garments, the hijood for sportswear and the burkini for swimwear, allowed Muslim girls to participate in activities at a level they may not previously have been able to.

The burkini has found an audience beyond the Muslim community, and while some people have differing opinions about the burkini, it can't be denied that it has given many girls and women access to sports and experiences they would have otherwise avoided because of health, body or religious concerns.

Aheda, with your flair for fashion and love of the Australian outdoor lifestyle, you've created garments that symbolise inclusion, leisure, fitness and health.

We like your style!

A SHOUT-OUT TO

ALICE ANDERSON

FOR JUMPING IN
THE DRIVER'S SEAT

A tip of the cap
to the girls who
think there's no
such thing as jobs
for the boys.

ALICE ANDERSON

(1897–1926)

Born in Melbourne in 1897, Alice Anderson grew up at a time of increasing female independence. In 1902 women were first given the right to vote around Australia, and then, with the outbreak of World War I, women were relied upon to take over many jobs that traditionally had been done by men.

However, women weren't encouraged to stay in these roles after the war was over and the men returned home. Alice wasn't having any of that! In 1916 at the age of 19, she became a driver for her father's company, transporting mail over the dangerous route from Healesville to Marysville. Alice quickly found her own unconventional niche as a chauffeur, taking Melburnians on weekend trips or picnics in the country. With her jaunty peaked cap, breeches and short hair, she became quite the celebrity driving around Melbourne in her eight-seat convertible touring car!

Alice soon became a fully qualified mechanic and a founding member of the Women's Automobile Club. In 1919 she opened her own business, Kew Garage, where she employed an all-female staff of mechanics and apprentices, teaching women how to drive and fix cars at a time when few had the opportunity to learn. Ever practical, Alice could often be seen working in her overalls and boots. She even invented a board on castor wheels to easily scoot under cars – similar to the ones mechanics still use today!

Alice, you not only found your drive in a career that women had been discouraged from entering, but you trained other women to follow in your footsteps.

We will always remember your pioneering attitude.

ILLUSTRATION BY SONIA KRETSCHMAR

A SHOUT-OUT TO
ANNETTE KELLERMAN
FOR HER DARING AND DETERMINATION

Cheers for the trailblazing women who challenge the norm, stay strong and never give up.

ANNETTE KELLERMAN

(1886–1975)

Born in Sydney, Annette Kellerman received swimming lessons early to strengthen her weak legs. Few would have guessed it would lead to an amazing career! Annette went on to become a women's swimming and diving record holder. She also excelled as a long-distance swimmer – a sport women hadn't competed in before. She swam the Yarra, the Thames and the Seine (where she was the only female competitor and placed third)! Annette was also the first woman to attempt to swim the English Channel. She was a force to be reckoned with!

Instead of wearing the heavy, skirted swimsuits of the day, Annette wore a one-piece costume, which was more practical for swimming. Annette's outfit was controversial, though – in 1907 she was arrested in Boston for indecency. This scandal helped change society's attitude towards beach fashion – for the better. Soon, Annette's one-piece bathing suit was the accepted female attire for the beach and pool.

Annette, nicknamed the Australian Mermaid, moved on from swimming to become a vaudeville artist and a silent film star, appearing in over ten Hollywood films.

Being a savvy businesswoman as well as an advocate for health, fitness and positive body image, Annette opened health spas and a health-food store, created exercise techniques and wrote books on women's health, fitness and beauty.

Annette, thank you for pushing boundaries and inspiring us in the area of fitness and health. Your can-do attitude shows us anything is possible.

We won't forget the way you broke new ground.

ILLUSTRATION BY CATHIE GLASSBY

A SHOUT-OUT TO
BETTY CUTHBERT
FOR RECORD-BREAKING ATHLETICISM

Rapturous applause for the amazing sportswomen whose dedication and class take their achievements across the finish line.

BETTY CUTHBERT

(1938-2017)

As an 18-year-old from Sydney, Betty Cuthbert won three gold medals at the 1956 Olympics in Melbourne. She surprised the world with her sprinting ability in the 100 metres, 200 metres and 4 x 100 metres relay track events. She was dubbed Australia's 'Golden Girl' for her swag of medals and her golden locks.

Betty's willpower led to an impressive comeback to athletics years later even though she'd suffered many injuries. Betty won gold in the 400-metre track event at the 1964 Olympics in Tokyo. Yes, that means she was a gold medallist in four different events!

When Betty was diagnosed with multiple sclerosis (MS) five years later, she was forced to retire from sport, but was honoured as a torchbearer at the opening ceremony for the 2000 Olympics in Sydney. Her strong spirit continued throughout her life, as she focused on raising the awareness of MS until her passing in 2017.

Betty's amazing achievements remain as her legacy. She's the only athlete in the world to have won gold in all three Olympic sprint events — 100, 200 and 400 metres. And she's the only Australian track athlete ever to have won four gold medals at the games. She was at the forefront of women's athletics and remains one of the best sprinters in Olympic history.

Betty, you captivated the nation with your spectacular sprinting and your story will continue to inspire Australian athletes for generations to come.

We hope to embrace our challenges with as much determination as you.

ILLUSTRATION BY CARLA McRAE

A SHOUT-OUT TO
CARRIE BICKMORE
FOR PUTTING BRAIN CANCER IN THE SPOTLIGHT

Put your hands together for the beneficent babes who are raising awareness and keeping hope alive.

CARRIE BICKMORE

(1980-)

Carrie Bickmore is the golden girl of Australian TV and radio. Her career and achievements so far are pretty impressive – from 'Carrie at the News Desk' on *Rove Live*, to Gold Logie winner and long-running host of *The Project*. All this aside, Carrie is as real and down-to-earth as they come.

Using her public profile, she often acts as an unofficial voice for those who don't hold the same power – and we love her for it. She is a dedicated humanitarian and devotes a lot of her time to many charities. But the cause that is closest to her heart is the charity she set up – Carrie's Beanies 4 Brain Cancer.

In her Gold Logie award acceptance speech in 2015 she courageously spoke about her personal experience with brain cancer. In 2010 her first husband died at just 34 years of age after a decade-long battle with the illness. Her honesty raised awareness of this devastating disease and the fact research in this field is severely underfunded. Carrie ended her speech encouraging Australians to wear a beanie the next day and to share a photo on social media.

From that moment the charity went from strength to strength and has raised over $1 million through community fundraising events, the sale of beanies and the BrainBeats concert.

In 2017 Carrie was named on the Victorian Honour Roll of Women in recognition of her work as a charitable and inspirational role model.

Carrie, your strength, hope and positivity has captured the heart of the nation and you have empowered young girls to be more charitable and fight for a cause.

We are head over heels for your beanies!

ILLUSTRATION BY EMMA LEONARD

A SHOUT-OUT TO

CATE BLANCHETT

FOR BEING AUSTRALIA'S
LEADING LADY

Let's toast
the superb
stars standing
centrestage and
speaking their
minds.

CATE BLANCHETT

(1969–)

Cate Blanchett was born and raised in Melbourne. Her passion for the performing arts was evident from a young age. After travelling overseas in her early twenties, she moved to Sydney and attended the National Institute of Dramatic Art (NIDA) to pursue an acting career. And what a career she has had!

With numerous acting accolades to her name including two Academy Awards, six AACTAs, three Golden Globes and three BAFTAs, Cate is used to being honoured for her acting talent. But her work in other parts of her life – heading arts organisations such as the Sydney Theatre Company, and supporting humanitarian and environmental causes – deserves equal celebration.

She has regularly used her high profile to draw attention to social and political issues, particularly environmental campaigns. She helped launch the Australian Conservation Foundation's 'Who on Earth Cares' campaign, which aimed to encourage Australians to lobby politicians on environmental matters, and was made an honorary life member of the Australian Conservation Foundation in 2012 in recognition of her outstanding support. In 2016 Cate was appointed as a global Goodwill Ambassador for the UN Refugee Agency.

Aside from being one of the most graceful and elegant women in the world, she is also intelligent, motivated and a great role model for women and young girls. As an active feminist, Cate has spoken passionately about women's rights and the pressures that women face in Hollywood to fit a certain mould.

Cate, your fierce pride in the Australian film and theatre industry and your exceptional charitable work has inspired and paved the way for our young performers.

We want to shine bright like you!

ILLUSTRATION BY LUCY ROLEFF

A SHOUT-OUT TO
CATHERINE MARTIN
FOR MAKING MOVIES SPECTACULAR

The award goes
to the women
who work behind
the scenes to
bring vision and
glamour to the
stage and screen.

CATHERINE MARTIN

(1965-)

Which Australian has won the most Academy Awards for making wonderful films? An actor? A writer? No – it's Catherine Martin, who has won four Academy Awards for designing and producing the sets and costumes of *Moulin Rouge!* and *The Great Gatsby*.

Catherine has spent her life admiring and creating beautiful objects. Growing up in Sydney, she loved to watch classic Hollywood movies, opera and ballet, and was entranced by the intricate costumes and sets. She got to experience old-world fashion in person too, through watching vintage fashion parades thrown by her grandmother. Catherine learnt how to sew and create patterns for clothes, and began to make her own original dresses.

She honed her skills in art school before studying design at the famed National Institute of Dramatic Art (NIDA). That's where she met her future creative and life partner, fellow student Baz Luhrmann.

Their first collaboration was the stage play of *Strictly Ballroom*, which was so successful that they turned it into a movie. With glitter, glam and sparkles aplenty, Catherine's elaborate design style caught the eye of the world and set the creative path for her future celebrated work.

Catherine's attention to detail is mesmerising and the results are always spectacular. In *Moulin Rouge!* and *The Great Gatsby*, Catherine's designs combine careful research into the historical setting, ravishing beauty and surprising modern elements. The blend of old and new allows viewers to feel as if they are inside 1900s Paris or 1920s New York as the stories unfold.

Catherine, your passion, hard work and knack of making the past feel fresh and dazzling has brought so much beauty and enjoyment to millions of people.

We admire your flair!

ILLUSTRATION BY ASTRED HICKS

A SHOUT-OUT TO
CATHY FREEMAN
FOR BRINGING A NATION TOGETHER

Stand up and roar
for our girls in the
green and gold!

CATHY FREEMAN

(1973-)

Cathy Freeman grew up in Queensland with her sister and three brothers. She started athletics training with her stepfather when she was very young and by her early teens had won an impressive collection of regional and national titles in both track and field events.

She always showed fierce determination and focus on the track. At 16 Cathy competed in her first major international event, the Commonwealth Games in New Zealand. Soon after, she moved to Melbourne, where she continued to build her career with the help of professional trainer Peter Fortune.

Cathy is perhaps best remembered today as the athlete chosen to light the flame at the 2000 Olympics in Sydney, and for her stunning win in the 400 metres. Have you ever jumped from your seat in sheer exhilaration as someone not only rises to a challenge but completely nails it? Australia did that day. Flying against convention, Cathy proudly carried both the Aboriginal and Australian flags in her lap of honour, staying true to herself as always.

Today, Cathy works tirelessly for the foundation she established, which helps kids in four remote Indigenous communities attend school and get the best out of their education.

Cathy, in your superwoman suit, you didn't need a cape to show us that skill, training and hard work are as essential as talent in gaining fantastic results. You have taught us that being a leader is as much about community and roots as success.

We'll always cheer you on!

ILLUSTRATION BY TORI-JAY MORDEY

A SHOUT-OUT TO

CONNIE JOHNSON

FOR AMAZING TENACITY AND SELFLESSNESS

Cheers to the
girls and women
who stare down
life's toughest
experiences and
turn them into
something that
helps others.

CONNIE JOHNSON

(1977-2017)

Connie Johnson was just 11 years old when she developed a rare type of bone tumour. She recovered but unfortunately developed cancer again at age 22. Connie recovered a second time, and went on to get married and have two sons. In 2010 when she was 33, Connie was diagnosed with breast cancer. Doctors believed she had less than a year to live.

Connie refused to give up. She might not survive cancer this time, but she would do all she could to help other women stay healthy and see their children grow up. That meant she needed people's attention.

Connie enlisted the help of her actor brother Samuel, and together they created the Love Your Sister foundation to raise money for cancer research and to encourage all the women of Australia to check themselves for signs of breast cancer. Samuel rode 15,000 kilometres around Australia – *on a unicycle*. He set a world record and Love Your Sister raised almost $2 million.

But why stop there? Connie's Big Heart Project was about small things making a big difference. Connie called for donations of five-cent pieces – and got millions of them. She created a massive heart shape out of five-cent coins, set a new record and raised another $2 million for cancer research.

The Love Your Sister foundation has raised more than $5.6 million for vital cancer research and encouraged millions of women to recognise the warning signs of breast cancer. In 2017 Connie was awarded a Medal of the Order of Australia.

Connie, you helped scientists keep searching, demonstrated unbelievable perseverance and inspired millions to keep striving come what may.

We're grateful to you for working so hard for so long.

ILLUSTRATION BY ALICIA ROGERSON

A SHOUT-OUT TO

DAISY PEARCE

FOR MOVING THE GOALPOSTS

Let's do a Mexican wave for the sports stars who are doing what they love and doing it well! Their feats are creating opportunities for generations of girls to come.

DAISY PEARCE

(1988-)

Daisy Pearce was born in Victoria and loved footy from a young age. The bounce of the red Sherrin was unpredictable and the way the players moved the ball around the field was so exciting. Daisy enrolled in Auskick and signed up for her school AFL team. At Bright Football Club she also played in the under-13s and under-15s teams, where she was the only girl.

Thinking that there was no way for her to continue playing AFL competitively, Daisy then tried her hand at volleyball. That was, until she was spotted in a school footy game. Before she knew it, she was playing for the Darebin Falcons in the Victorian Women's Football League.

Since then, Daisy hasn't stopped kicking, marking and tackling. She is now the captain of Melbourne Football Club in the AFL Women's Competition – the team mascot is even named after her! And in the AFLW's first season she won the Players' Best Captain award and was named All-Australian team captain. Off the field, Daisy made history as the first woman to call the football in Triple M's 21-year history of commentating the game. Move over, lads!

Daisy is also a qualified midwife – only hanging up her surgery gloves for footy boots in 2016.

Daisy, you're a champion player and a first-class role model for our sporty sisters, and you're inspiring girls across Australia and the world to play like a girl.

We dream to one day kick goals like you!

ILLUSTRATION BY CARLA McRAE

A SHOUT-OUT TO

DHARMICA MISTRY

FOR HER EXCITING MEDICAL BREAKTHROUGH

Raise your
beakers to the
young scientists
revolutionising
modern medicine.

DHARMICA MISTRY

(1987-)

Dr Dharmica Mistry is a scientist who made a remarkable discovery that could help save lives all over the world. After completing her Bachelor degree, majoring in Microbiology, Dharmica went on to investigate the association between breast cancer and hair. She would regularly use her own hair as a control when testing the hair of patients. One day, Dharmica observed that her hair was showing the same features as the hair of a breast cancer patient. After being given the all clear, Dharmica's eureka moment was when she realised that she had recently used oil to moisturise her hair.

This revelation led Dharmica to discover that oils from the blood of breast cancer patients were being deposited in their hair. This indicated that a simple blood test could screen for the disease. Dharmica is now working hard to bring this test to the Australian market, which would revolutionise the way women living in remote areas access breast cancer testing.

For this groundbreaking research, Dharmica was awarded the title of 2015 Young Scientist of the Year. In 2016 Dharmica was announced as Young Executive of the Year by the *Australian Financial Review* and was also the recipient of the NSW Young Woman of the Year award, for which she was nominated by the Minister of Health, Jillian Skinner.

Dharmica, your intelligence and dedication to your research is extraordinary, and you're inspiring girls to don a lab coat and use their skills to help improve the lives of others.

We can't wait for women to benefit from your discovery!

ILLUSTRATION BY GEMMA FLACK

A SHOUT-OUT TO
EDITH COWAN
FOR FIGHTING FOR EQUALITY

Hip hip hooray for
the trailblazers
who forge
new paths,
break barriers
and don't let
convention stand
in their way.

EDITH COWAN

(1861–1932)

Edith Cowan was born in 1861 at Glengarry, near Geraldton, Western Australia. At a time when women did not attend universities or have the right to vote, she was a political force to be reckoned with. Edith quickly developed her political reputation in the 1880s. She was involved in many organisations including the founding of the Karrakatta Club, Australia's first women's social club. Edith was also a member of the suffragette movement which saw women in WA granted the right to vote in 1899.

Edith was foremost community-minded, and during World War I she was chairperson of the Red Cross Appeal Committee. In 1920 she was appointed to the Order of the British Empire for her contribution to the war effort. In the same year, a Bill was passed in WA giving women the right to run for parliament. Edith jumped at the opportunity and in 1921 was elected to the Legislative Assembly of Western Australia as a member of the Nationalist Party, becoming Australia's first female parliamentarian – a dream come true for our stalwart suffragette!

Edith's most notable achievement in parliament was her contribution to the passing of the Women's Legal Status Bill, which opened legal and other professions to Western Australian women for the first time.

Up until her death in 1932, Edith championed women's rights, migrant welfare, social justice and infant health. Since 1995 Edith's portrait has been printed on the $50 note in celebration of her exceptional achievements.

Edith, you're a pioneer of our modern society and you're inspiring girls across Australia and the world to improve their communities and aspire to higher ideals.

We salute your devotion and drive!

ILLUSTRATION BY MARCELA RESTREPO

A SHOUT-OUT TO
ELIZABETH BLACKBURN
FOR MAKING BIG DISCOVERIES

Shiny medals for
all our science
luminaries who
are improving our
lives every day
with research,
experimentation
and beakers full
of brainpower.

ELIZABETH BLACKBURN

(1948-)

Elizabeth Blackburn was born in Tasmania and from a young age loved animals and nature – she even kept tadpoles in glass jars at home. Elizabeth was so inspired when she read Marie Curie's biography that she went on to study science and now holds a Bachelor of Science, a Master of Science and a PhD from Cambridge University, plus a wealth of other awards and honours for her work in various scientific fields.

But her biggest achievement is winning the Nobel Prize in Physiology or Medicine. Along with two colleagues, Elizabeth was awarded the prize in 2009 for her discovery of the enzyme telomerase. It's pretty complicated, but the enzyme impacts our telomeres, which are the caps at the end of each strand of DNA that protect our chromosomes. In short, telomeres are vital to our health and how quickly we age, so this finding was very important. Elizabeth is the first Australian female Nobel Laureate – Marie Curie would be proud!

With a Nobel Prize in her lab coat pocket, Elizabeth went on to serve on the President's Council for Bioethics in America for two years. In 2017 she published a book, *The Telomere Effect: A Revolutionary Approach to Living Younger, Healthier, Longer*, and is currently the president of the Salk Institute for Biological Studies in California.

Elizabeth, your curiosity and research has changed our lives, and you're inspiring girls in Australia and across the world to ask questions and find answers.

We are captivated by your scientific mind.

ILLUSTRATION BY SYLVIA MORRIS

A SHOUT-OUT TO

ELLA HAVELKA

FOR HER TENACITY ON
AND OFF THE STAGE

Give a standing ovation to the girls who work hard, overcome obstacles and take life into their own hands.

ELLA HAVELKA

(1989–)

Ella Havelka is a dancer with the Australian Ballet who never gave up on her dreams. A descendant of the Wiradjuri people, Ella was raised by her mother, Janna. An active child, Ella took her first ballet class at age seven, after seeing a glimpse of *Swan Lake* on an old video tape.

Ella continued to dance, working hard until she won a place at the Australian Ballet School in Melbourne. When Ella graduated, however, she wasn't invited to join the Australian Ballet. Instead, she joined the Bangarra Dance Theatre, where she had to learn a whole new style of dance. Ella didn't let this get her down, though, and perfected the contemporary and cultural style.

In 2013 Ella was accepted into the Australian Ballet, making her the first Indigenous dancer since the company was founded in 1962. Returning to the more classical style of dance took a lot of hard work, but Ella persisted. Since joining the Australian Ballet, Ella has toured nationally and internationally, won an *Instyle* Women of Style Arts and Culture Award, and fulfilled a lifelong goal of dancing in *Swan Lake*.

When her pointe shoes are off, Ella continues to express her artistic nature through painting, lino-cutting and practising traditional Aboriginal basket weaving.

Ella, you're an inspiration to young dancers and dreamers everywhere, showing that persistence pays off and teaching girls to pursue their dreams.

We admire your grace and talent.

ILLUSTRATION BY KRISTY DREISE

A SHOUT-OUT TO
FELICITY WISHART
FOR STANDING FIRM

An ocean of
gratitude for
those who
protect our
natural world
so that future
generations may
appreciate it.

FELICITY WISHART

(1965–2015)

Felicity Wishart had five brothers, so she grew up knowing how to stand up for herself. She was a teenager when she joined the protests to save Tasmania's Franklin Dam, and like many others she was arrested and briefly jailed. The Franklin Dam protests were a pivotal moment in Australia when people power stopped the proposed construction of a dam that would have destroyed a treasured World Heritage Area forever.

After Felicity graduated university with a Bachelor of Science in Environmental Studies, she began working at the Australian Conservation Foundation, successfully campaigning for the beautiful wet tropical rainforests of North Queensland to be World Heritage listed.

Throughout her career Felicity worked with grace and resolve to protect our priceless natural wonders. She campaigned for the plight of tropical rainforests in the Asia-Pacific region, worked to stop land clearing in Queensland, shaped strategies to combat climate change, and fought for a national network of marine protected areas to be created.

Felicity was an inspirational leader in Australia's environmental movement, who recognised the importance of training young activists, as well as supporting the talent of others. Felicity and her fellow campaigners at the Australian Conservation Foundation, the Queensland Conservation Council, The Wilderness Society and the Australian Marine Conservation Society have shown us that courage, tenacity and passion can be enough to change the world.

Felicity, you cared so deeply for the environment that you dedicated your life to its care and protection.

We won't let your legacy be forgotten, and we'll continue the fight.

ILLUSTRATION BY EVI OETOMO

A SHOUT-OUT TO
FIONA WOOD
FOR SAVING LIVES

Don your scrubs
for the devoted
doctors and
surgeons who
dedicate their
lives to curing
illness, helping
victims of tragedy
and easing pain
and suffering.

FIONA WOOD

(1958–)

When she was young, Dr Fiona Wood dreamt of being an Olympic sprinter, but it was another career – medicine – which would see her become an inspiration to so many. After studying in London, Fiona was drawn to plastic surgery, which soon led her to the burns unit, and so her passion in this field was born.

In 1987 Fiona migrated to Australia with her family and settled in Perth, where she completed her medical training. In 2002 tragedy struck with the Bali bombings and Fiona was thrust into the spotlight when a group of injured survivors were sent to Royal Perth Hospital. Leading a team and working around the clock, Fiona helped to save 25 patients with severe burns. Thanks were certainly in order – a Medal of the Order of Australia, that is.

In 2003 Fiona was named Australian of the Year, and from 2005 to 2010 she was voted Australia's Most Trusted Person – even if we didn't know there was such an honour, Fiona certainly deserves it! Awards aside, one of Fiona's biggest accomplishments is her development of 'spray-on skin', which is a world-first technology used to treat burns.

Fiona continues to undertake new research in the field of burns medicine and every day her findings are making a difference to people's quality of life.

Fiona, your integrity, intelligence and ingenuity have made you a hero to so many. You're helping and healing the world in a very special way.

We trust you completely!

ILLUSTRATION BY AMANDA BURNETT

A SHOUT-OUT TO

GERMAINE GREER

FOR DEMANDING TO BE HEARD

Let's show some love for the feisty feminists who are tearing down stereotypes and smashing taboos.

GERMAINE GREER

(1939–)

Germaine Greer was born and raised in Melbourne. An incredibly intelligent young woman, she immersed herself in academia by attending the University of Melbourne, the University of Sydney *and* Newnham College, Cambridge – pretty smart, hey? It was throughout these defining student years that Germaine became attracted to radical feminist politics, which paved the way for her famous involvement in the second-wave feminist movement of the 1960s.

Her greatest accomplishment, and biggest contribution to feminism, came in 1970 with the publication of her first book, *The Female Eunuch*. Considered extremely controversial at the time, it was a call to women to raise the roof and take on the world. She pushed against the boundaries placed on women, and inspired young women to strive for liberty.

Her work didn't stop with feminist issues: she has gone on to debate everything from Indigenous rights to literature and the environment. She is scrappy, outspoken and undeniably controversial, but there is no getting around the fact that she was and remains a brave and passionate advocate of liberty for women.

Germaine, your unbreakable self-confidence, unashamed intelligence and occasionally outrageous attitude has been inspiring young women around the world for decades, to stand up, speak out and challenge the ideals of what it means to be a woman.

We want to stand up like you!

ILLUSTRATION BY ELIN MATILDA ANDERSSON

A SHOUT-OUT TO

ITA BUTTROSE

FOR BOLDLY TAKING ON THE MEDIA INDUSTRY

We salute the women who don't just wave the flag for us, but pave the way in male-dominated industries.

ITA BUTTROSE

(1942-)

As a young woman of just 23, Ita Buttrose was appointed women's editor of the *Telegraph* — quite the accomplishment! After a brief stint in the UK, Ita returned to Australia in 1971 to become founding editor of *Cosmopolitan* magazine before joining forces with Frank Packer to launch a rival publication, *Cleo*. Both *Cosmo* and *Cleo* pushed boundaries for women in terms of their content and, with Ita at the helm, provided information that was topical and entertaining.

Ita successfully juggled life as a mother with a career at a time when there was little infrastructure to support pregnant women in the workplace. In fact, it was more common for women to stop work completely to undertake 'domestic duties'.

Ita's business relationship with media mogul Frank Packer would prove to be a long and productive one, as she went on to be editor of the *Australian Women's Weekly* and Publisher of the Australian Consolidated Press Women's Division. In 1981 Ita was lured by Rupert Murdoch to News Limited where she became the first female editor of a major metropolitan newspaper in Australia and was appointed to the board.

With a groundbreaking career, Ita has maintained the respect of both men and women across all sectors of the media industry and continues to work in television today.

Ita, you are a generous and warm woman who has shown us how to manage a career with both dignity and integrity, and you are inspiring young girls to chase their dreams.

We are in awe of your verve.

ILLUSTRATION BY CAITLIN SHEARER

A SHOUT-OUT TO

JADE HAMEISTER

FOR EXPANDING
OUR WORLD VIEW

Clear a path for the insatiable adventurers whose life-embracing outlook is encouraging us to fight for positive social and environmental change.

JADE HAMEISTER

(2001–)

Jade Hameister's love of adventure was kicked into gear on a trip to Mount Everest Base Camp when she was just 12 years old. Along with her adventurer father, Jade began planning her arctic expedition as soon as she returned home to Australia. First up was skiing to the North Pole – at this point Jade didn't even know how to ski! But with fierce training, planning and incredible willpower, Jade became the youngest person in history to ski to the North Pole.

Her next big adventure was to travel to the other side of the globe to trek across the world's second largest icecap – the Greenland crossing. Strength and sheer determination saw Jade succeed where others couldn't. Next up for Jade is reaching the South Pole. If she can complete this final, incredibly difficult journey, she will become the youngest person to ever achieve the polar hat-trick! But for Jade it's not about breaking records, it's about doing something she loves and learning every step of the way – about our world and also about herself.

In turn, Jade has been inspired to share what she has learnt with others. Her TEDx Talk has been watched thousands of times. In it, she encourages young girls to aim higher, to focus on what they can do rather than how they look, and to help protect our planet. In 2016 Jade was named the Australian Geographic Society's Young Adventurer of the Year.

Jade, your appetite for adventure has enabled you to travel far and wide and share your world view with so many. Because of your actions and words, girls around the world will believe there really are no limits.

We are motivated by your adventures!

ILLUSTRATION BY CAT MacINNES

A SHOUT-OUT TO

JESS GALLAGHER

FOR HOLDING FAST TO HER DREAM

Gold medals for
all the wonderful
women who
strive to succeed,
whatever the
barrier.

JESS GALLAGHER

(1986–)

Jess Gallagher was always passionate about sport. In her teens she played state-level netball and basketball, but in her last year at school, she discovered she had a rare eye disease and lost 90 per cent of her sight. Instead of holding her back, her disability made her even more determined. She set herself the goal to represent Australia in sport and to win a medal in both a Summer and Winter Paralympics or Olympics.

Jess began a gruelling training regime and was chosen to represent Australia in athletics at the 2008 Summer Paralympics, only to be ruled ineligible due to being 0.01 per cent too sighted in one eye. Undaunted, she switched to alpine skiing and became the first female Australian to medal at a Winter Paralympics, winning bronze in the Women's Slalom with her guide Eric Bickerton at Vancouver in 2010.

She missed out on medals in the 2012 Summer Paralympics because of injury but was back in shape for the 2014 Winter Paralympics, where she won bronze in the Giant Slalom with guide Christian Geiger.

Jess switched to track cycling, and won a bronze medal with her pilot rider, Madison Janssen, in the one-kilometre time trial at the 2016 Rio Paralympics. Jess had achieved her dream and what no other Australian had done before.

Jess has also become a qualified osteopath and a motivational speaker. She's a board director and ambassador for Vision 2020 Australia, and an ambassador for Disabled Wintersport Australia and Visions Australia/Seeing Eye Dogs Australia.

Jess, despite everything you had to face, you found a way to achieve your dreams. You have inspired us to persevere with our goals.

We are blown away by your amazing achievements!

ILLUSTRATION BY CAT MacINNES

A SHOUT-OUT TO
JESSICA WATSON
FOR CONQUERING THE WORLD

Here's to the
ordinary girls with
extraordinary
dreams.

JESSICA WATSON

(1993-)

Jessica Watson blasted onto the world stage in 2010 when, at only 16, she successfully sailed solo nonstop and unassisted around the world in her yacht, *Ella's Pink Lady*. It was a 210-day journey, which involved travelling 23,000 nautical miles over some of the world's most challenging oceans.

Jessica grew up in a family passionate about boats and even lived on one for five years of her childhood, and yet she was afraid of the water, shy, quiet and anything but adventurous. But when she was read the story of Jesse Martin's solo sailing trip around the world at only 17, it hatched a dream, and over the next few years Jessica threw herself into learning as much as she could about boats, sailing and the sea.

Those years of preparation would help Jessica survive not only the intense loneliness of long days alone on the ocean, but also terrifying moments when her boat was knocked sideways into the water in huge seas.

As her adventure unfolded, the world followed through her blog. It attracted five million hits on the day she sailed back into Sydney, where she was overwhelmed by a crowd of 75,000, including the Australian Prime Minister.

Jessica went on to become Young Australian of the Year in 2011, was awarded a Medal of the Order of Australia in 2012, wrote a book about her experiences, filmed a documentary with Sir Richard Branson, skippered the youngest ever crew to compete in the Sydney to Hobart Yacht Race and is now a co-founder and Communications Manager of a start-up company, Deckee.com.

Jessica, you proved to the world that if you believe in your dreams, and work hard, you can overcome any obstacle.

We are in awe of your fearless nature!

ILLUSTRATION BY JESSICA SINGH

A SHOUT-OUT TO

JESSIE STREET

FOR CHAMPIONING HUMAN RIGHTS

Our deepest
admiration for
the unshakeable
dedication of
the women who
devote their lives
to improving ours.

JESSIE STREET

(1889-1970)

Born in India, Jessie Street moved to Australia as a child when her mother inherited a cattle property. Her passion for creating change started early – at university, Jessie was already campaigning for women's sport facilities, and when she visited England after graduation, her first political action was to join suffragette demonstrations.

Jessie was determined to improve the status of women and help to bring social justice, equal rights, an end to discrimination, and peace to all.

In the 1930s she founded the United Associations of Women, tackling the sources of the economic inequalities she saw during the Great Depression. During World War II she went undercover to experience what conditions were like as a worker at a munitions factory, as well as fronting up at Parliament House in Canberra to argue for servicewomen to receive equal pay with men.

In 1945 Jessie was the only woman on the Australian delegation to the conference that founded the United Nations. Jessie was our first representative on the UN Economic and Social Council Commission on the Status of Women. In the 1950s and 1960s she campaigned overseas with the World Peace Council for nuclear disarmament.

Jessie visited remote Indigenous communities, and fought for equal access to social services for Indigenous families. Jessie's suggested amendments to the Australian Constitution to remove discrimination against Indigenous people became law in the 1967 referendum.

Jessie, you never stopped working for causes that needed a champion. We still have a way to go with achieving equality, but with you as our role model . . .

We're up for the challenge!

ILLUSTRATION BY EVIE BARROW

A SHOUT-OUT TO

JORDAN RASKOPOULOS

FOR BEING TRUE TO HERSELF

Our sincerest
thanks to the girls
who show the
world the whole
of who they are.

JORDAN RASKOPOULOS

(1982-)

Jordan Raskopoulos is one of Australia's most sought-after comedy performers and an internationally acclaimed comedian, both in her own right and as part of the musical comedy group, Axis of Awesome. She has received fistfuls of television credits and is an Australian National Theatresports champion. Undoubtedly talented, her skits will have you in stitches!

Jordan was known for much of her career as a man, before she let her outside become an expression of her inside. She came out as transgender in a 2016 video by Axis of Awesome called 'What's happened to Jordan's beard?' that went on to become viral.

Taking the gamble on being true to herself at the height of her career can't have been easy, but since then, Jordan has become an increasingly important role model. She's continued to use her personal brand of humour to promote awareness and understanding of LGBTQIA+ people, and has spoken out about the importance of understanding mental health in her 2017 TEDx Talk.

Today, Jordan continues to bring us joy as a comedian, and provides a positive, vocal role model for anyone experiencing gender dysphoria.

Jordan, you're a powerhouse who's proved that the biggest risks can give the greatest rewards, and that we should always be true to ourselves.

We are proud of you for being YOU!

A SHOUT-OUT TO

JULIA GILLARD

FOR SHOWING US THAT NO JOB IS OUT OF REACH

A round of
applause for the
girls who inspire
us to shatter the
glass ceiling and
rise to the top.

JULIA GILLARD

(1961–)

Julia Gillard was born in the United Kingdom and came to Australia when she was five. She found her passion for politics at university and graduated from Melbourne University with an Arts/Law degree. She took a job with a major law firm, where she worked with trade unions to speak up for workers and protect their rights. Her determination and intelligence meant that she found success in this largely male-dominated environment.

In 1996 Julia resigned from her prominent position as a lawyer and went on to pursue a career in federal politics. Julia was always fiercely supportive of women and this shone through in her early political endeavours. As a member of the Australian Labor Party, she helped draft the party's Affirmative Action rules to boost the number of women in the ALP. She was also a founding member of EMILY's List Australia, which was created to support female political candidates.

It wasn't long before Julia was working her way up the political ladder. She held her own as Deputy Prime Minister and she was strong, decent and outspoken as Minister for Employment and Workplace Relations, Minister for Education and Minister for Social Inclusion. By 2010 Julia was in Australia's top job – she was our 27th Prime Minister and the first woman to lead our country.

Julia retired from politics in 2013 and published her hugely successful political memoirs, *My Story*. She is still a passionate voice for social good, chairing the boards of the mental health organisation beyondblue and the Global Partnership for Education.

Julia, you've shown us that with perseverance, intelligence and confidence we can be leaders in every way.

We aspire to lead like you!

ILLUSTRATION BY CAITLIN SHEARER

A SHOUT-OUT TO
JUSTINE FLYNN
FOR COMBINING BUSINESS VISION AND SOCIAL JUSTICE

Let's put our arms around the movers and shakers in the business world who are creating and innovating with a social conscience.

JUSTINE FLYNN

(1977-)

Together with her now-husband, Daniel Flynn, and their friend Jarryd Burns, Justine dreamt up a company that would use its profits to help others. They'd noticed that Australians bought lots of bottled water, even though tap water is safe and virtually free. Not everyone has easy access to clean drinking water. What if the trio sold bottled water and donated the profits to projects that made clean water more accessible in developing nations?

The group persevered with their idea and Justine's creativity and outside-the-box thinking were essential to the success of their company. Thankyou sells water, body care and food products, and donates 100 per cent of its profits. It funds projects that provide safe water, food, and hygiene and sanitation services to communities around the world.

Along the way, Justine's work has been recognised in many ways – she was a finalist in the 2014 Telstra Women's Business Awards, was one of *Marie Claire* magazine's 30 Women Changing the World in 2015, and due to the empowering environment she created at Thankyou, the company won Employer of the Year at the 2015 *Food Magazine* awards.

Now a mum – or should that be supermum? – Justine has used her insights to launch the Thankyou baby range, which helps get child and maternal health programs to families in need.

Justine, you've changed the lives of many by never taking anything for granted and always pushing for change. You've shown us that something as simple as a bottle of water has the power to combat poverty.

We want to thank YOU!

ILLUSTRATION BY BINNY TALIB

A SHOUT-OUT TO
KYLIE KWONG
FOR DREAMING BIG BUT ACTING LOCAL

Wave your chopsticks in the air for our culinary queens, who, with a dash of this and a sprinkling of that, promote sustainable food and ethical eating.

KYLIE KWONG

(1969-)

Kylie Kwong is one of Australia's leading chefs and has crafted an impressive career based on her family's culture and her commitment to sustainably sourced produce. As a third-generation Australian, Kylie was just five years old when she started to learn (from her mother) about the southern Chinese heritage of the food they had at home — how to cook, eat and share it.

In 2000 Kylie opened her own restaurant in Sydney, Billy Kwong. Here, she had the freedom to reinterpret Cantonese cuisine and showcase her love of fresh, seasonal and organic produce, with a strong focus on Australian native ingredients. Kylie is an active supporter of the sustainable food movement, and is dedicated to promoting a more environmentally friendly, community-minded and healthier attitude to where we buy and how we cook our food.

Her advocacy of sustainability also extends to her involvement with community organisations including the Stephanie Alexander Kitchen Garden Foundation, Oxfam and Half the Sky Foundation. On Sundays, Kylie has a stall at Carriageworks Farmers Market in Sydney, where she gives back to the community by spruiking the message of awareness in growing, buying, cooking and eating fresh and local food.

Her unique contribution to the food world has been recognised internationally, and in 2014 she was named one of *Fortune* magazine's influential Women in Food.

Kylie, thank you for keeping our bellies full and our tastebuds delighted! You have opened our eyes to the importance of locally grown food and native produce.

We can't wait to see what else you will serve up!

ILLUSTRATION BY NGAIO PARR

A SHOUT-OUT TO
LAYNE BEACHLEY

FOR HER STRENGTH AND COMPETITIVE SPIRIT

Yell loud and long
to thank the girls
who ride the
waves and strive
for greatness.

LAYNE BEACHLEY

(1972-)

Born in Manly, Sydney, Layne Beachley grew up with the ocean in her blood. From a very early age, Layne wanted to be the best at something. Once she settled on surfing, her focus and dedication led her to become the first surfer, male or female, to win six consecutive world surfing titles. She won seven in total, as well as almost 30 other tour competitions.

This success came through hard work and perseverance. A professional surfer by 16, Layne sometimes worked up to four jobs at a time to raise the money needed to travel the world surfing circuit. As a result, she understands how difficult it can be to follow your dreams. In 2003 Layne started her foundation, Aim for the Stars, to help financially support young women in their quest to achieve their goals.

Retiring from surfing hasn't slowed Layne down. In 2009 she was a state finalist for NSW Australian of the Year, and in 2011 she was inducted into the Sport Australia Hall of Fame. She was named Officer of the Order of Australia in recognition for her community and charitable works in 2015, as well as being appointed chairperson of Surfing Australia. She's also an author, motivational speaker and role model!

Layne, thanks for following your dreams and never giving up. You inspire us and we have no doubt that you'll keep achieving!

We love your energy and determination.

ILLUSTRATION BY FREDA CHIU

A SHOUT-OUT TO

LISY KANE

FOR LEADING
WOMEN FORWARD

Here's to the
women in tech
who are breaking
new ground and
celebrating the
sisters they meet
along the way.

LISY KANE

(1987–)

Melbourne-based Lisy Kane is a games producer, entrepreneur and all-round go-getter. After growing up playing video games, Lisy built her life around her passion and studied to join this typically male-dominated field. She's come a long way since her days of renting consoles from her local library! The games she's produced – including *Armello* (League of Geeks) and *Hand of Fate* (Defiant Development) – have been highly successful, garnering awards, huge pre-release excitement and legions of loyal fans.

But Lisy's not only a leading games developer – she's also someone who is passionate about helping others find their way in the industry she loves. To help raise the profiles of women in gaming and technology, Lisy co-founded the Girl Geek Academy, a start-up that encourages women to break into the tech industry and launch their own businesses. The talented Girl Geeks run workshops and hackathons, and are building a community of fantastically geeky girls.

It's this can-do, celebratory attitude that stands out about Lisy – and the world agrees. She's the recipient of the 2017 Tim Richards Award, a 2016 Film Victoria Women in Games Fellowship, and she was on the 2017 *Forbes* '30 under 30' gaming list. We're sure there are many more accolades to come.

Lisy, you're an awesome role model, fostering community and creativity, and inspiring gaming, coding, tech-loving girls everywhere.

We can't wait to get our geek on with you!

A SHOUT-OUT TO

LOUISE MACK

FOR WRITING FROM THE FRONT LINE

An honorary
salute to the
stout-hearted
sisters who share
their stories
so others can
experience the
world through
their eyes.

LOUISE MACK

(1870-1935)

Louise Mack was born in Hobart, the seventh child in a family of 13. The Macks moved around a lot before settling in Sydney when Louise was 12. A spirited and charming girl, Louise was an engaging storyteller from a young age.

She wrote her first three novels while in Australia, and a column called 'A Woman's Letter' in the *Bulletin*. In 1901 she moved to London and wrote the novel *An Australian Girl in London*, which led to a job offer at the British newspaper the *Daily Mail*.

With the outbreak of World War I in 1914, Louise's career took on a new, exciting and rather dangerous turn. Living in Belgium at the time, Louise became a war correspondent – Australia's first female war correspondent. Unswayed by the danger of the front line, Louise armed herself with a portable typewriter and documented the awful truths of defeat – this girl had guts! When she lost communication with London she was unable to send news reports, so instead kept a journal recording the atrocities she saw.

By 1915 Louise was back in England and, using her detailed journal, she wrote and published *A Woman's Experiences in the Great War*. Louise donated most of the profits from her books sales to The Red Cross to help Belgian refugees.

Louise, your adventurous spirit led you to use your experiences to create amazing works of fact and fiction. You have inspired us to realise the power of the pen.

We could read your stories all day long!

ILLUSTRATION BY LILLY PIRI

A SHOUT-OUT TO

MAGDA SZUBANSKI

FOR HELPING US LAUGH
AND SPEAKING THE TRUTH

Brava for the women who make their own roles on stage, on screen and in life.

MAGDA SZUBANSKI

(1961–)

Magda Szubanski was born in the United Kingdom, and grew up in Melbourne. At university, Magda and her friends staged comedy shows. News of the talented group spread and they were invited to create a show for the ABC. Their sketch show, *The D-Generation*, was hugely popular on TV and on radio.

From there, Magda kept writing and performing comedy. In 1995 Magda teamed with fellow comedians Jane Turner and Gina Riley to write, perform and produce *Big Girl's Blouse*. All-female comedy shows were a rare sight on TV, and this one spawned characters that became international phenomenons.

Jane and Gina created the hit sitcom *Kath & Kim* in 2002. Magda joined them to play Sharon Strzelecki, and her reputation as one of Australia's most loved comedy writers and actors was cemented. Sharon showcased Magda's keen ear for how people speak and think, and her ability to make her underdog characters endearing and relatable.

While Magda spent decades in the public eye, she kept her life private. In 2015 she published her memoir, *Reckoning*. She wrote about the difficult times in her relationship with her parents, her experience of anxiety and depression, her struggle with her weight, and her fears that coming out as gay would make friends, family or audiences turn away from her. Today, Magda is vocal in her support for LGBTQIA+ issues and encourages young people to be hopeful and true to themselves.

Magda, your comic creations have brought laughter to millions of us, and through your honesty and advocacy you are an inspiring voice.

We want to be as funny, accomplished and compassionate as you.

ILLUSTRATION BY JORDYN McGEACHIN

A SHOUT-OUT TO
MARITA CHENG
FOR BRINGING THE FUTURE CLOSER

Let's hear it for
the bold and
brainy girls who
are using science,
technology,
engineering and
maths (STEM) to
take us towards a
bright future.

MARITA CHENG

(1989–)

Marita Cheng grew up with her mum in Cairns, Queensland. She graduated from high school in the top 0.2 per cent of Australia for her year. That same year, Marita was named Cairns Young Citizen of the Year.

But it's what she's done since that has really wowed us. While Marita was studying Mechatronics and Computer Science at university, she founded Robogals, an organisation that encourages young women to study engineering and related fields. Since 2008 Robogals has taught robotics workshops to more than 50,000 girls in more than ten countries. And in 2012 Marita was named Young Australian of the Year for her work at Robogals.

Marita didn't stop there. She's gone on to become a technology entrepreneur, starting her own company, aubot (formerly 2Mar Robotics), researching and building robots that help us in our everyday lives. In particular, Marita's company designs robotic aids, such as Teleport, which can be used by people with limited mobility, kids with cancer, and the elderly. Marita also co-founded Aipoly, whose first app recognises objects in real time and describes what it sees to help people who are visually impaired or colourblind understand their surroundings.

Marita, you've achieved so much in such a short time, and you're inspiring girls across Australia and the world to be engineers, robotics designers, entrepreneurs and technology advocates.

We can't wait to see what you do next!

ILLUSTRATION BY ELIN MATILDA ANDERSSON

A SHOUT-OUT TO
MARY MACKILLOP
FOR HER CHARITY AND DEVOTION

Our heartfelt
thanks to the girls
who devote their
lives to helping
others no matter
the hardships.

MARY MACKILLOP

(1842-1909)

Mary MacKillop, the oldest of eight children, left home at a young age to help provide for her family. In her late teens she travelled to Penola, New South Wales, to teach her uncle's children. Mary was passionate about education being available to everyone and opened her classroom to any child wanting to learn – even if they couldn't pay.

Mary's Catholic faith was strong and she decided to devote herself wholly to others. In 1867 with the help of her friend, Father Tenison-Woods, she renamed herself Sister Mary of the Cross, took a vow of poverty and co-founded the first order of nuns in Australia – the Sisters of Saint Joseph of the Sacred Heart.

Mary and the Sisters opened many schools and other charitable organisations. But they came up against difficulties with some church leaders. Mary fought hard for the Sisters' right to retain control of the order, and was even excommunicated at one point. Soon reinstated, Mary continued to care for those who needed help: children, women and families who were struggling with poverty, unemployment and illness.

In 2010 Sister Mary was officially canonised, making her Australia's first saint.

Mary, you were a fierce advocate for your fellow sisters
and a champion for education and social justice.
Your legacy lives on and will continue to teach girls
the importance of kindness and charity.

We are overwhelmed by your compassion and strength!

ILLUSTRATION BY AMANDA BURNETT

A SHOUT-OUT TO

MARY
REIBEY

FOR NEVER
GIVING UP

Here's to the
gutsy girls who,
with grit and
determination,
survive and
thrive against the
odds, making us
believe anything
is possible.

MARY REIBEY

(1777–1855)

Mary Haydock was an orphan from Northern England. At 13 she was sent to work as a house servant. It didn't last long. Mary ran away, disguised herself as a boy and stole a horse. She was arrested and put on trial.

You could say Mary was lucky. Horse theft was punishable by death, but Mary's sentence was commuted to seven years' transportation to the young colony of New South Wales. She made the frightening six-month journey aboard a convict ship and arrived in 1792.

After two years in Sydney and repeated proposals, 17-year-old Mary married Thomas Reibey. Thomas was granted land and established farms and other ventures, and the couple had seven children.

When Mary was 34, Thomas died. As a woman and a former convict, Mary was looked down upon by many powerful people. But Mary didn't sell up or fade into the background. She had run the family businesses whenever Thomas had travelled, so Mary worked towards expanding them. She became a respected member of the growing colony, an advocate for free education, and she helped found the Bank of New South Wales, the first bank in Australia (now Westpac).

Mary, you were a survivor and a force to be reckoned with, and your experiences show girls that they can change their destiny.

We admire your get-up-and-go!

ILLUSTRATION BY STELLAR LEUNA

A SHOUT-OUT TO

MAY EMMELINE WIRTH

FOR FLYING HIGH
AND FREE

A standing
ovation for the
daring dames
whose courage
and strength
know no limits
and who inspire
us to seize every
opportunity.

MAY EMMELINE WIRTH

(1894-1978)

May Emmeline Wirth was born in Bundaberg, Queensland. Her mother was Australian while her father was a circus rider from Mauritius. At age six, May's parents separated and she was adopted by Mary Wirth, an equestrian and sister of the Wirth brothers, who owned one of Australia's largest circuses. By then May was already turning somersaults, or 'flip-flaps' as they were called!

Soon May was featuring in balancing, tumbling and contortionist acts, and wowing crowds with her breathtaking tightrope walks. She learnt equestrian skills from her adoptive mother and at age ten started to perform tricks in the circus shows on bare horseback. 'Roll up! Roll up! To see the "fearless hurricane hurdle rider",' the ringmasters cried. May was short but strong and flew through the air with the greatest of ease.

Before she was 20, May visited America, where she was invited to tour with the world-famous Barnum & Bailey circus. May was an immediate success and she delighted the crowds with tricks such as leaping from the ground onto the back of her galloping horse and somersaulting backwards through rings. May continued to travel the world performing, before retiring in 1937 and settling in America. May's name now lives on in the Circus Hall of Fame.

May, you were an audacious performer and embraced everything life had to offer. You're inspiring girls across Australia and the world to move forward with heads held high.

We are dazzled by your feats!

ILLUSTRATION BY FREDA CHIU

A SHOUT-OUT TO

MELINA MARCHETTA

FOR BEING THE VOICE
OF A GENERATION

Grazie di cuore
to the smart
signorine who put
their heart and
soul on the page
to create our
fictional BFFs.

MELINA MARCHETTA

(1965-)

Melina Marchetta is a third-generation Italian-Australian who grew up in Sydney's Inner West. She first made her mark on the publishing scene when her debut novel, *Looking for Alibrandi*, was published in 1992. It was a story that spoke to a whole generation and was a stellar success. *Alibrandi* is still extremely popular today, showing just how much readers appreciate having honest stories about women's culturally based experiences.

As a writer, Melina can put her mind (and pen) to anything: she has written YA fiction, epic fantasy and even contemporary crime. Whatever genre she is writing, her stories always centre on identity and the importance of family and community. She writes in such a way that her characters become a part of you – you can't help but connect with them, their authenticity and their rawness.

Among a whole host of awards, she has received the Children's Book Council of Australia Book of the Year Award for *Alibrandi* and for her second novel, *Saving Francesca*. She also won the American Library Association's Michael L. Printz Award for Excellence in Young Adult Literature for *On the Jellicoe Road*. Her books have been published in 18 countries and in 17 languages. And to top it off, *Alibrandi* was made into an award-winning feature film – not bad for a chick from Marrickville!

Melina, with your beautifully descriptive prose and characterisation, you have captured the hearts of readers for more than 20 years.

We can't wait for the next generation to pick up your books too!

ILLUSTRATION BY ZOE CARACATSANOUDIS

A SHOUT-OUT TO

MOLLY TAYLOR

FOR GOING
FULL THROTTLE

Let's give
first-place
ribbons to the
thrill-seekers
and speed
demons for
persevering and
succeeding
in previously
male-dominated
sports.

MOLLY TAYLOR

(1988–)

Molly Taylor was born into a motorsport-mad family, with both her parents having been rally car drivers. But it wasn't cars that first interested Molly, it was horses. She competed at national level in various equestrian events, and it wasn't until working at her father's rally school one holiday that she tried driving a rally car herself.

After that, Molly was hooked. It was time to trade her horses for horsepower! Initially she borrowed a friend's car to compete in local events, where she had impressive results. Then, upon getting her rally car licence, she started to race professionally. She won back-to-back Australian Rally Championships in the F16 class. Molly then headed off to Europe to chase her dream. With very little money, she leased a car and worked on it herself.

All the hard work paid off, with Molly becoming one of the youngest and the only female driver participating in the 2011 World Rally Championship. On returning to Australia, Molly began competing in the Australian Rally Championship in the overall classification. In 2016 Molly and her team took out the series, making Molly the first female and youngest-ever driver to win the title. When she's not driving rally cars at breathtaking speeds, Molly works with various organisations to encourage more women to try motorsports.

Molly, you've chased your dream across the world, achieving so many 'firsts' at such a young age, and you're inspiring girls to take control of the wheel.

We respect your drive!

ILLUSTRATION BY GEMMA FLACK

A SHOUT-OUT TO

MUM SHIRL

FOR UNWAVERING DEDICATION AND GENEROSITY

Thanks are not enough for the advocates and activists who give so much of themselves to help others in need.

MUM SHIRL

(1924–1998)

Mum Shirl, originally named Colleen Shirley Perry, was an Aboriginal woman of the Wiradjuri people and grew up in Cowra, New South Wales.

When her brother was imprisoned, Shirl went to see him regularly. After he was released, she kept visiting so that she could help other prisoners. When officials asked why she was there, she'd say 'I'm his mum', and the nickname 'Mum Shirl' stuck. For a while, officials gave her a pass to prisons all around NSW so that she could keep seeing those who needed her.

Mum Shirl was renowned for giving her time and her money, even though she didn't have much, to those who needed it. As well as visiting prisoners, she would go along with people to court, to help them understand the unfamiliar and intimidating legal system. Sometimes people who might have gone to prison were given another chance because Mum Shirl spoke up for them.

In the 1970s Mum Shirl's tireless work became more political and official. She helped guide the men and women making the Gurindji land rights claim, and helped to create the first Aboriginal Legal Service and Aboriginal Medical Service and other community and political groups.

Her work was commemorated with a Medal of the Order of Australia and an Order of the British Empire. A plaque in Redfern, where she did so much of her work, celebrates the life of 'the black saint of Redfern who gave aid and comfort to all who asked'.

Mum Shirl, you spoke up for those who didn't have a voice and improved the lives of so many.

We hope we can be as brave and determined as you were.

ILLUSTRATION BY KATE MOON

A SHOUT-OUT TO

NANCY WAKE

FOR KICKING THE GESTAPO'S BUTT!

Here's to the fearless femmes who can face the world at its worst and strive for change.

NANCY WAKE

(1912–2011)

Nancy Wake's story starts in 1912 in Wellington, New Zealand, far away from the war-torn Europe where she made her mark. Nancy and her family moved to Sydney, Australia, in 1914.

As a teenager Nancy longed to see the world. So when she received £200 from a relative, she hopped on a boat and moved to London and then Paris, where she worked as a journalist. In 1935 during an assignment in Vienna, Nancy witnessed the impact of the Nazi regime first hand. The horrifying scenes made Nancy determined to fight the Nazis and led to her courageous role in the French Resistance.

Nancy was a force to be reckoned with: she helped to spirit over a thousand escaped prisoners of war out of France and through to neutral Spain. Her valiant contribution did not go unnoticed by the Nazis — she soon became number one on the Gestapo's most wanted list. They named her the 'White Mouse' due to her ability to elude capture.

With a price on her head, Nancy escaped to London, where she trained as a spy. When she completed her training, she parachuted back into France. Her job was to supply the Resistance with weapons and establish covert communication with bases in England. On one occasion she cycled 500 kilometres in 71 hours to re-establish a coded wireless communication network. Her focus was rock-steady to the end of her epic journey, when she wept in pain and relief.

Nancy, you saved countless lives and fought against oppression and persecution with courage and strength in the face of impossible odds.

We will never forget your bravery.

ILLUSTRATION BY SYLVIA MORRIS

A SHOUT-OUT TO

NORA HEYSEN

FOR PAINTING OUR HISTORY

Let's celebrate our artistic treasures who, with passion, skill and dedication, create enduring masterpieces and defy the boundaries of their fields.

NORA HEYSEN

(1911-2003)

Nora Heysen was born in South Australia and raised in a historic home in the Adelaide Hills. She was one of eight children and her father, Hans Heysen, was a famous landscape painter. At a young age Nora decided that she too would like to be a painter. To get to art classes in Adelaide, she walked to the station and then took an hour-long train journey – what a trooper! At home she had to milk the cows in the morning and in the evening, but all her spare time was set aside for painting.

In her twenties Nora had her first solo exhibition and then went to London to study and paint. When she came back to Australia she moved to Sydney, and in 1938 she became the first woman to win the Archibald Prize, Australia's biggest prize for portraiture. It was another 22 years before a woman took out the prize again.

During World War II Nora again made history by being the first woman appointed as an Australian war artist. Hello, Captain Heysen! She painted women in the army, air force and navy and made over 170 artworks during this time. Apart from her portraits, Nora also painted many floral arrangements and still life scenes. It is said that Nora painted more self-portraits than any artist except Rembrandt.

Nora, you were a gifted artist with unwavering commitment to your craft, and you're inspiring girls across Australia to embrace creativity and paint their stories.

We want to bring the world to life like you!

ILLUSTRATION BY KIATA MASON

A SHOUT-OUT TO

OLIVIA NEWTON-JOHN

FOR SHINING A LIGHT
ON BREAST CANCER

Let's sing the
praises of the
multitalented
entertainers
who bring us so
much joy and
use their profiles
to champion
important issues.

OLIVIA NEWTON-JOHN

(1948-)

Olivia Newton-John was born in England but moved to Australia with her family when she was five. A singer from a young age, Olivia got her big break when she won a talent contest on TV. The prize was a trip to London, which set Olivia on the road to stardom. She recorded her first record there and has since gone on to sell over 100 million albums.

But Olivia did more than just sing. She will forever be remembered for her role as Sandy in the hit film *Grease*, in which she acted alongside John Travolta. If Olivia's star was already shining brightly, this movie shot it into another stratosphere – it was like greased lightning! Olivia continued to act, sing, record and perform around the world, as well as becoming more involved in humanitarian causes.

Olivia was the first Goodwill Ambassador to the United Nations Environment Programme and has held many other spokesperson and ambassador roles. In 1992 Olivia was faced with her own battle when she was diagnosed with breast cancer. With strength and honesty, Olivia spoke publicly about her struggle and became an inspiration to millions of others fighting the disease. Olivia is passionate about raising cancer awareness and improving breast health. To this end, she established the Olivia Newton-John Cancer and Wellness Centre, which provides cancer care and research.

Olivia, your dedication to cancer research and your inherent positivity has given those in need strength, hope and invaluable support.

We are hopelessly devoted to you!

ILLUSTRATION BY SARAH BOESE

A SHOUT-OUT TO

OODGEROO NOONUCCAL

FOR PAVING THE WAY

Stand aside for the thinkers and creatives who challenge the system for the sake of what's right.

OODGEROO NOONUCCAL

(1920–1993)

Oodgeroo Noonuccal was an Indigenous poet and activist. She was known as Kath Walker until 1988 when she changed her name to Oodgeroo (meaning paperbark) of the Noonuccal people. Born on Minjerribah (North Stradbroke Island), Oodgeroo was heavily influenced by her father, who campaigned for better conditions for Indigenous workers in Queensland.

Her poetry collection *We Are Going* (1964) was one of the first books to be published by an Indigenous woman and it sold out several editions. Oodgeroo was one of the highest selling Australian poets of her time. She made an amazing contribution to Australian literature with several works of poetry, non-fiction and stories for children published throughout her lifetime.

Oodgeroo was also an active campaigner for Indigenous rights and social justice. She was a member of several organisations that were important in establishing equal voting rights and citizenship for Indigenous Australians (granted in 1965 and 1967). On Minjerribah, Oodgeroo also set up the Noonuccal-Nughie Education and Cultural Centre, a place for visiting students to learn about Indigenous culture, history and environmental conservation.

Oodgeroo, you were one of many who fought for basic rights for the traditional owners of this country. Your beautiful poetry and focus on cultural learning inspires us to work towards a better future.

We hope we can make a difference to our country, like you.

ILLUSTRATION BY LEANNE TOBIN

A SHOUT-OUT TO
QUENTIN BRYCE
FOR HER LEADERSHIP AND DEDICATION

Applaud the
girls who go
first, create
opportunities and
champion others
to follow.

QUENTIN BRYCE

(1942–)

From an early age, Quentin Bryce dreamt of making the world a better place. With this idea firmly in mind, she went on to achieve remarkable things in her career – many of them firsts for women.

Quentin was one of only two women studying Law at her university in the 1960s and became one of Australia's first female barristers. She was also the first woman to be appointed to the University of Queensland's Law School, where she taught for many years. And this was just the beginning of her amazing career! Among many leadership posts, she was named the Federal Sex Discrimination Commissioner in 1988 and served as Governor of Queensland from 2003 to 2008 – only the second woman to do so. And then came the 'first' that made her a household name: in 2008 she became the first female Governor-General of Australia. In 2014 Quentin was made a Dame of the Order of Australia, in recognition for her work in this role.

She is still a tireless advocate for human rights with a focus on women's rights. A devoted letter-writer, Dame Quentin keeps in contact with people from all walks of life. She is passionate about people connecting and looking after each other within their communities.

Quentin, thank you for paving the way for women in the areas of law, politics and public service. Your commitment to making our nation the best it can be is inspiring.

We love your vision and compassion!

ILLUSTRATION BY ALICIA ROGERSON

A SHOUT-OUT TO
RACHEL PERKINS

FOR BRINGING INDIGENOUS STORIES TO THE SCREEN

Here's to the fearless women who use the richness of their creativity to show us that everyone's stories matter.

RACHEL PERKINS

(1970-)

Rachel Perkins was born in Canberra, and is from the Arrernte and Kalkadoon people. She is the daughter of famous activists Eileen and Charles Perkins, who always told her she could make a difference and change the world.

Rachel started a traineeship in film at the Central Australian Aboriginal Media Association in Alice Springs when she was 18, and at 21 became the youngest female executive producer at SBS Television. She then founded a production company called Blackfella Films, won an Indigenous Program Scholarship at the Australian Film Television and Radio School in Sydney, joined the ABC as executive producer of their Indigenous Programs Unit, and began a career making award-winning films featuring Indigenous actors and stories.

Rachel's first feature film was *Radiance*, which tackled issues such as the Stolen Generations, racism, abuse and adoption, and won many awards at festivals around the world. She followed this with the multi-award-winning *One Night, The Moon* with Paul Kelly, and has since directed the films *Bran Nue Dae*, *Mabo* and *Jasper Jones*, and co-created the TV series *Redfern Now*.

Rachel is passionate about empowering others and using art to 'change hearts'. She is the founder, director and curator of the Message Sticks Indigenous Film Festival; a co-founder of National Indigenous Television (NITV); and is committed to letting her people speak for themselves through storytelling of all kinds.

Rachel, you've worked tirelessly to tell the stories of Indigenous people and Australia's rich cultural heritage. You've shown us that with intelligence, passion and skill, girls can be creative powerhouses in every way.

We treasure your talent to tell our nation's stories.

ILLUSTRATION BY KRISTY DREISE

A SHOUT-OUT TO

ROSIE BATTY

FOR HER COMPASSION AND BRAVERY

Here's to the courageous and strong women who speak out for the vulnerable.

ROSIE BATTY

(1962–)

Rosie Batty was born in the United Kingdom, and came to Australia in 1988. She began to campaign for domestic violence victims in 2014. She opened up to reporters not long after her son's death at cricket practice on a suburban sports oval in Melbourne, and impressed everyone with her determination to give a voice to victims of domestic violence despite her own tragedy. Luke was just 11 years old when he became a victim at the hands of his father, but Rosie calmly and with compassion told her story to the world and showed us how domestic violence can affect anyone, no matter how rich or poor, or how educated or smart they are. In doing so, she has helped convince Australian governments that more needs to be done to recognise and prevent abuse within families.

Rosie was Australian of the Year in 2015, and in that year she also published her moving and inspiring memoir, *A Mother's Story*. She continues to speak out publicly whenever she can, calling for change and raising money for the Luke Batty Foundation to help women and children affected by domestic violence.

Rosie's incredible strength and selfless efforts inspire other people who have experienced abuse to speak out and act. Her bravery and outspokenness have helped improve many people's lives.

Rosie, your courage and empathy have helped the discussion of family violence take centrestage in Australia. You've shown us that, with compassion and courage, girls can champion victims and give them a voice, making a difference to everyone's future.

We aspire to be as brave as you.

ILLUSTRATION BY ANNA MAY HENRY

A SHOUT-OUT TO

SIA

FOR SINGING PROUDLY AND DOING THINGS HER OWN WAY

Sing it for the sisters who bring us so much joy through music.

SIA

(1975-)

Music and art have always been a big part of singer-songwriter Sia Furler's life. She grew up in Adelaide, where her mother was an art lecturer and her father was a jazz musician. She moved to London to pursue a music career and then to the United States. After some success and some disappointments, her popularity bloomed.

But touring and constantly being in the public eye became exhausting. Sia thought her job was to write songs and perform; the media seemed to think her job was to have every part of her life watched and criticised. She stopped performing and concentrated on writing songs for other singers, including Beyoncé and Rihanna. Sia's songs were everywhere – even if she wasn't singing them herself.

Sia never wanted to be famous and to this day still doesn't, but she wasn't going to let that get in the way of doing what she loved most. How could she keep writing and performing her music but stay a private person? The eternal visual creative, Sia hit on a genius and simple way of keeping her face hidden to maintain her anonymity, keep her audience intrigued and all the while allow her talent to shine through in performances. Her face-shielding platinum blonde wig has become almost as synonymous with the singer as her spine-tingling voice, but has allowed her to keep part of herself out of the public eye. The media might still be paying attention to how Sia looks instead of how she sounds, but she has taken back a little bit of control over what can be seen.

Sia, your talent and determination to forge a career that makes you happy is awesome. You are teaching girls that it is possible to maintain your privacy and sense of self in this celebrity-crazed world.

We can't wait to see what you create next.

ILLUSTRATION BY EVIE CAHIR

A SHOUT-OUT TO
STELLA YOUNG
FOR KEEPING IT REAL

Here's to the women who speak up to make life better for everyone.

STELLA YOUNG

(1982–2014)

Stella Young grew up in the country town of Stawell, Victoria. She was born with a genetic condition called osteogenesis imperfecta, which she described as having 'dodgy bones'.

After studying Media and Education at Deakin University, Stella worked as a teacher, educator, journalist and award-winning comedian. As well as hosting *No Limits*, a disability culture program on community television, Stella was the editor of the ABC's *Ramp Up* online magazine, which gave a voice to disability issues in Australia.

Stella wrote and spoke with honesty, humour and warmth, challenging our perceptions and making us think. In particular, Stella wanted us all to know that people with disabilities want to be seen as individuals like everyone else does, and they aren't necessarily 'brave' or 'courageous' simply for going about their everyday lives. And Stella's 2014 TEDx Talk titled 'I'm not your inspiration, thank you very much', delivered with her signature deadpan wit, made the world pay attention – it's since been watched almost 2.5 million times.

Stella, thank you for your disability advocacy and social justice activism, for making us laugh, for keeping it real, for changing the way we think, and for getting us to take action.

We miss your fierce, funny and brilliant voice.

ILLUSTRATION BY SANDRA ETEROVIĆ

A SHOUT-OUT TO
TURIA PITT
FOR BEING A SURVIVOR

Let's make some noise for all the lion-hearted ladies whose strength and courage know no bounds.

TURIA PITT

(1987–)

Turia Pitt was born on the tropical island of Tahiti. Her family migrated to Australia when she was three years old and settled on the New South Wales south coast.

In 2011 Turia entered an ultra-marathon race through the Kimberleys that would change her life forever. She was caught in a grassfire and suffered extreme burns to over 65 per cent of her body. Doctors gave her only the slimmest chance of survival. She endured six gruelling months in hospital, underwent over 200 operations and spent two years in recovery. Despite being told she'd never walk again, Turia defied all expectations by painstakingly rebuilding her life and her fitness.

Renowned for her pure grit, indomitable spirit and passion for humanitarian work, she has refused to let the fire define her and has gone on to thrive in the ultimate story of triumph over adversity.

Her achievements are mind-blowing. As an ambassador for Interplast, she has walked the Great Wall of China, the Inca Trail and Kokoda Track. Through these walks she raised almost $1 million in donations to help people in developing countries gain access to reconstructive surgery. She is also an extremely successful motivational speaker and has created a goal-setting initiative called School of Champions. And if that wasn't enough – in October 2016, she competed in the Ironman World Championships in Hawaii. GO TURIA!

Turia, your bravery, strength and determination are out of this world! Your unstoppable spirit has shown girls around the globe that it is possible to surpass the seemingly impossible.

We are bowled over by you and your passion for life.

ILLUSTRATION BY EVIE BARROW

A SHOUT-OUT TO

VALI MYERS

FOR CRAFTING A UNIQUE
AND CREATIVE LIFE

Wild cheers for the women who dare to defy convention and show that there is more than one way to live a rich and fulfilling life.

VALI MYERS

(1930-2003)

It seems Vali Myers always knew that the familiar path was not for her. She left home young and worked in factories so she could pay for dance lessons. While still a teenager she was lead dancer in the new Melbourne Modern Ballet Company, then left for Paris to pursue a career.

But Paris, like much of Europe, was still recovering from World War II in 1949. Vali struggled to find work, and at times she lived on the streets. In the city's bohemian nightclubs, Vali was known for her wild dancing, charisma and startling appearance. Dutch photographer Ed van der Elsken captured the era and his version of Vali in his 1954 book, *Love on the Left Bank*.

After Paris, Vali lived in an isolated valley in Positano, Italy, where she turned her home into a wildlife sanctuary and developed her visual art. Her work is often called 'fantasy' or 'visionary' art, as she sought to capture her personal and spiritual world. Animals, especially her beloved fox, feature in many of her works.

Whether she was in Paris, Positano or visiting New York to sell her art, Vali was a magnet and muse for other artists, writers and musicians. She valued creative, honest people, but had little interest in celebrity and fashion.

In her later years, Vali moved back to Melbourne, and ran a studio in the beautiful Nicholas Building. Vali died in 2003, but designers and stylists continue to mimic her distinctive look, while her own art and diaries are held in collections in Australia and around the world.

Vali, your lust for life, freedom and creativity lives on in your art and the work you inspired.

We aspire to be as fearlessly true to ourselves as you were to yourself.

ILLUSTRATION BY SONIA KRETSCHMAR

A SHOUT-OUT TO
VIVIAN BULLWINKEL
FOR HER REMARKABLE STRENGTH AND RESILIENCE

Sound the horn
for the brave
women who
go above and
beyond to serve
their country in
times of war.

VIVIAN BULLWINKEL

(1915–2000)

Sister Vivian Bullwinkel was a courageous World War II army nurse and is remembered for her incredible story of service and self-sacrifice. Vivian was born in Kapunda, South Australia, in 1915. When she was 25 years old, she enlisted in the Australian Army Nursing Service.

Vivian was assigned to the 13th Australian General Hospital and sailed for Singapore. As the war intensified, the Allies were forced to evacuate. Vivian and 64 other Australian nurses boarded the *SS Vyner Brooke* but the ship was sunk by enemy aircraft. Vivian made it to shore, only to be the sole survivor of the Banka Island massacre, when Japanese soldiers shot 22 army nurses on Radji Beach, in February 1942.

After hiding in the jungle for several days, Vivian bravely surrendered and was taken prisoner. She survived in the prisoner-of-war camps of Sumatra for three and a half years. Despite the harsh conditions, Vivian was resilient and determined to return home to tell her story.

After the war, Vivian honoured the memory of her fallen colleagues by remaining active on veteran, nursing and philanthropic committees. Thanks to her, the events on Banka Island will not be forgotten.

Vivian's honours include being awarded the Florence Nightingale Medal and the Royal Red Cross Medal, as well as being appointed an Officer of the Order of Australia and Member of the Order of the British Empire.

Vivian, you were a true force of nature, and you're inspiring girls across Australia and the world to resist and rise above adversity.

We admire your unbreakable spirit!

ILLUSTRATION BY SAMANTHA BATTERSBY

A SHOUT-OUT TO

YASSMIN ABDEL-MAGIED

FOR STEPPING UP AND SPEAKING OUT

Here's to the
clever and
courageous girls
who can do
it all — fiercely
holding their own
on oil rigs,
in boardrooms
and in the media.

YASSMIN ABDEL-MAGIED

(1991–)

Yassmin Abdel-Magied was born in Sudan and grew up in Australia from the age of two. At 16 she founded Youth Without Borders, an organisation that empowers young people to work together to create change.

Yassmin has been appointed to various advisory groups and boards, including the board of DFAT's Council for Australian-Arab Relations. She has been the winner of numerous awards, including becoming a State Finalist for Young Australian of the Year at only 19 and a National Finalist at 23. Her tireless advocacy for youth, women and Australians from culturally and linguistically diverse backgrounds has made her a hero to many.

Yassmin's depth and determination have also seen her forge a career in the largely male-dominated Australian oil industry. After completing a Bachelor of Mechanical Engineering with First Class Honours from the University of Queensland, she worked for many years as a drilling measurement specialist and well-site engineer. In 2015 she was named as one of the Top 100 Most Influential Engineers in Australia by Engineers Australia.

As well as writing for local and international publications, representing Muslim Australians in social commentary, appearing on high-profile television programs and speaking widely on radio, Yassmin has hosted a documentary on racism, a motorsports podcast and the ABC's *Australia Wide* program. Her TED Talk 'What Does My Headscarf Mean to You' has been hugely successful, and she has already published her autobiography, *Yassmin's Story*.

Yassmin, you're inspiring young women everywhere
to speak without fear, push forward in the sciences and
be fearless advocates for social change.

We are motivated by you to shout out
and make our voices heard!

ILLUSTRATION BY EVI OETOMO

A SHOUT-OUT TO
YOU!

A million thanks
to all the girls
and boys who
have picked
up this book
wanting to learn
about awesome
Australian
women.

SARAH BOESE

LUCY ROLEFF

SONIA KRETSCHMAR

ASTRED HICKS

CATHIE GLASSBY

TORI-JAY MORDEY

CARLA McRAE

ALICIA ROGERSON

EMMA LEONARD

GEMMA FLACK

MARCELA RESTREPO

CAITLIN SHEARER

SYLVIA MORRIS

CAT MacINNES

KRISTY DREISE

JESSICA SINGH

EVI OETOMO

EVIE BARROW

AMANDA BURNETT

JORDYN McGEACHIN

ELIN MATILDA ANDERSSON

BINNY TALIB

NGAIO PARR

FREDA CHIU

LILLY PIRI

STELLAR LEUNA

ZOE CARACATSANOUDIS

KATE MOON

KIATA MASON

LEANNE TOBIN

ANNA MAY HENRY

EVIE CAHIR

SANDRA ETEROVIĆ

SAMANTHA BATTERSBY

Acknowledgements

Shout Out to the Girls was inspired by the awesome women of Australia and the continuing dialogue about how to acknowledge the lives of amazing women from around the world.

As a predominantly female team, Penguin Random House Australia Young Readers were excited to join the conversation and use our publishing expertise to shine light on the women of Australia who deserve to be recognised and celebrated.

As you can imagine, it was almost impossible to choose which of Australia's talented, brave, individual and groundbreaking women to include, and the book is by no means a comprehensive list – we're sure you can think of many women who could be among these pages!

We had no shortage of wordsmiths in our team offering to write about the women who personally inspired us, and a special shout-out goes to our writers: Amy Thomas, Claire Catacouzinos, Heather Curdie, Holly Toohey, Holly Willsher, Jessica Owen, Kimberley Bennett, Kristin Gill, Lindsey Hodder, Mary Verney, Michelle Madden, Susie Gibson, Victoria Stone and Zoe Walton.

This book wouldn't have been possible without the incredible illustrators who jumped on board with such enthusiasm and whose gorgeous artwork exceeded any of our expectations. A big shout-out to all of you!

Another shout-out needs to go to the book's incredible designer, Astred Hicks, whose creativity and patience knows no bounds.

Finally, we know there's still a way to go in achieving equality, but we are grateful to the families, carers, teachers, mentors and friends who are helping the next generation to grow up believing in and working towards equality for all.

A SHOUT-OUT TO

THE SMITH FAMILY

FOR HELPING DISADVANTAGED KIDS TO THRIVE AT SCHOOL

THE SMITH FAMILY

Founded 1922

All royalties from sales of *Shout Out to the Girls* will be donated to The Smith Family.

The Smith Family is Australia's leading children's education charity. It helps disadvantaged young Australians to succeed at school.

In Australia today there are 1.1 million children living in poverty.* The effects of family hardship go beyond a child's home life – it also affects their schooling. Without the things they need for school or access to additional outside-of-school support, disadvantaged children can fall further and further behind their classmates.

Not being able to keep up at school can lead to a child becoming disengaged from their learning. And without the skills or qualifications they need for a job, these young people will end up with poorer life outcomes overall.

However, investing in the education of a disadvantaged child delivers long-term positive benefits for them, their family and potentially generations to come. With Australians' support, The Smith Family is helping children in need to fit in at school, keep up with their peers and build aspirations for a better future for themselves.

*ACOSS Poverty Report, 2016

Shout-outs and massive thankyous to The Smith Family for helping kids all across Australia get the most out of their education.

Readers, thank you for buying this book and supporting The Smith Family's wonderful work.

DESIGNER'S NOTE

The Australian flora on the cover symbolises the strength and heart of the women featured in the book. Australian flowers aren't wilting violets; they are strong and tough, and have evolved to endure extreme environments. They are not flouncy and pretty, yet they still hold beauty in their structured and resilient nature.

#SHOUTOUTTOTHEGIRLS